ADVENTURE INTO CHRISTMAS

Experience the Wonder of Christmas with Jesus

by Beverly Bekker

ADVENTURE INTO CHRISTMAS
Experience the Wonder of Christmas With Jesus

Beverly Bekker 2023

First published by Beverly Bekker 2023

www.showtellgive.com

Printed by IngramSpark
ISBN: 978-0-6456320-2-6
ISBN Ebook: 978-0-6456320-1-9

*Dedicated to
every child whose imagination
lights up when reading these stories.
May you know Jesus and His
GREAT love for you.*

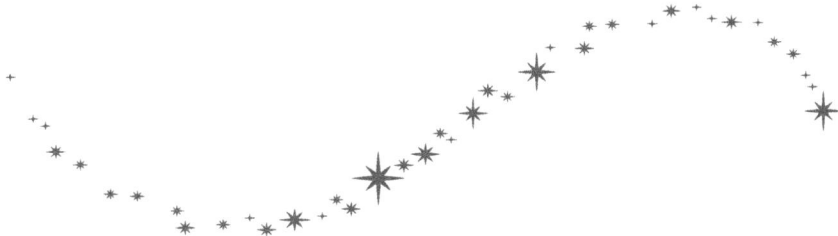

ACKNOWLENDGEMENTS

Thank you Roselyn Owen, my friend and partner in ministry, who sparked the idea for this book and helped with editing and design.
Thanks also to my husband, Anton, and my friend Ruth Reading, for your help with editing.

CONTENTS

Introduction

Dear Parent

Thank you for taking the time to read to your children. What a wonderful gift you are giving them!

Christmas is a time of "Wonder." And by "wonder," we refer to the sense of awe, curiosity, and amazement that envelops us during this festive season. Taking a moment to explain this to your children will help create a sense of anticipation before you "wonder" through the stories with them.

Each of these stories is based on the Christmas story in the Bible. You may want to read the story from the Bible first, and then read the immersive story I have written, to your child.

Each story begins with my encouragement to your child to 'Imagine'. To help them do this, I would like to suggest reading the following paragraph to them, or use your own words to prepare them to engage with the story:

It's time for you to quieten your heart and mind. Take a few deep breaths, get comfortable, sit or lie down quietly and close your eyes. God is with you now and He wants to be with you as you read the story.

If you choose to, you can imagine you are the character in the story, as I suggest, but of course you are free to imagine you are any other character in the story; or maybe you just want to listen and imagine the story unfolding, like a movie.

Imagine the sounds, sights, smells, feelings and even the tastes in the story. Your creativity and imagination are welcomed as you read or listen to the story.

When the story ends, you might want to read it again. Maybe you'll notice something or someone the second time that you didn't notice the first time. When you are finished reading or listening to the story, you can move on to the section I have called 'Talking Time'. In this section you can think and talk about your answers to the questions, even add your own questions, and talk with Jesus about what He wants to share with you about the story.
Maybe even draw or write your thoughts as you chat with Him.

I hope that you will have fun on your adventures with Jesus into the wonder of Christmas.

MARY GET'S
SURPRISING NEWS

Luke 1:26-38

Imagine.

You and Mary are friends, and you go over to her house for a visit. You are sitting together on your favourite, comfy couch. You know that Mary is thinking about Joseph who she is soon going to marry. She is so excited and can't wait for her wedding day. You are just about to get a snack from the kitchen, when you hear a soft noise. Mary hears it too and you both sit up straight.

The room is getting lighter and lighter. Suddenly the room is filled with a bright light, and the most beautiful, bright and BIG angel appears and he stands in front of Mary and looks at her with his bright eyes full of love. "Hallo Mary", he says in a kind voice. You wonder how Mary feels now. She looks amazed and confused at the same time. You know that she doesn't know what's going on and she looks over at you, her eyes wide with amazement.

You slide over to Mary and hold her hand. The angel leans closer and says, "Don't be afraid, Mary, for the Lord your God is so pleased with you. He is delighted with you and has chosen to surprise you with a wonderful gift. You will become pregnant and have a baby boy and you are to name him Jesus. He will be very great. He is the Son of God. He will reign as a King forever."

Mary grips your hand tighter. She lifts her head and says, "How can this be? I don't have a husband?"

The angel answers, "The Spirit of God will fall upon you and Almighty God will spread His shadow of power over you in a cloud of glory. This is why the child born to you will be holy. This is a promise from God himself. His promises are full of his power; nothing is impossible for God"

Mary is quiet for a moment. There are soft tears running down her cheeks, and she lifts her head and with a small smile she says, "This is amazing! I will be the mother of the Lord".

Mary lets go of your hand, climbs off the couch and kneels before the angel. "As His servant, I accept whatever He has for me. May everything you have told me come to pass."

The angel smiles and gently lays his hand on Mary's head and then he disappears.

The room is quiet again. You look at Mary.

There is so much to talk about, but for the moment you are both too surprised and shocked to say anything.

Talking Time

What did it feel like when the angel appeared?

What do you think Mary felt when the angel said God was pleased with her?

What would you feel and think if an angel came into your room?

Ask Jesus, if He sent you an angel with a message, what would it be?

Draw a picture of this story and put yourself in it.

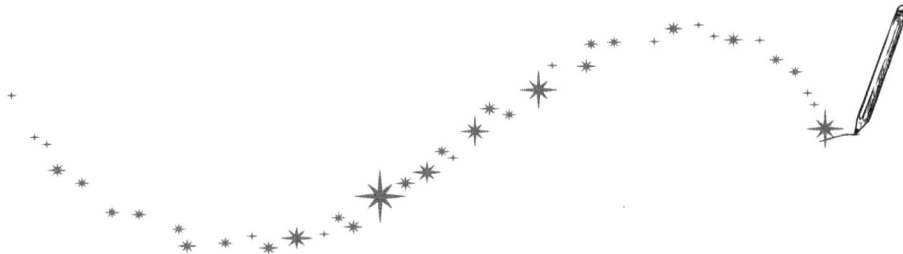

JOSEPH HAS A DREAM

Matthew 1:18-25

Imagine.

You are Joseph's helper in his workshop. Joseph is a carpenter. He has been working hard all morning and the workshop smells amazing. You have just finished sweeping all the wood chips off the floor. Joseph is making a beautiful table for Mary, his fiancé. The fine wood dust is making you sneeze.

Someone bursts into the workshop!
Looking around for Joseph and not finding him, he rushes over to you and asks, "Where is Joseph? I have urgent news to tell him."
"He's in the kitchen making himself some lunch", you answer quickly.

The man rushes into the kitchen and you hear him talking intensely to Joseph. After a lot of talking, the man says he must go now, and as he leaves you see he is very worried.

You strain your ears, but you can't hear anything more coming from the kitchen. You cautiously tiptoe over to the door and peek around the corner. Joseph is sitting on the floor with his head in his hands and he is crying and praying and talking to himself all at the same time. The man must have told him some very bad news. Joseph is crying out to God and asking him what to do.

"How can I take Mary to be my wife?", He cries out, "She is pregnant, which means she must love someone else!"

Eventually he makes a decision, "I will have to break it off with her. But I will do it quietly, so that no one knows. I love her too much to put her to shame... Yes, that's what I will do."

As Joseph sits there on the floor of the kitchen, weeping, you quietly go over and finish making his lunch. As you go over to give it to him, you realise that, because he is so exhausted from the shock of the news, he has fallen asleep.

While Joseph is sleeping, you decide to eat his lunch. It would be a shame to waste it! You're sure he won't mind.

Munching away on the sandwich, you can hear Joseph talking in his sleep. He must be dreaming!

Just as you're about to start on the second sandwich, Joseph suddenly wakes up.

Jumping to his feet, Joseph looks over at you, grabs the left-over lunch and starts to laugh.

"I can marry Mary after all! You'll never believe what just happened!"

You are pleased that Joseph is happy again, and seems to have solved his problem after getting the bad news.

He explains, "I just met an angel of the Lord in a dream while I was sleeping. He told me not to worry, but to take Mary as my wife since she is pregnant because of the power of the Holy Spirit. She doesn't love somebody else! I don't know how this has happened, but I will trust God and do as the angel has told me."

Rushing out to the door, Joseph turns around, grabs you by the shoulders and with a huge, beaming smile says, "The angel told me that Mary is going to have a baby boy! And we are to name him Jesus! He is the one the world has been waiting for. He has been sent by God to save us!"

And with that Joseph disappears out the door.
You are left feeling out of breath and amazed.

Talking Time

Have you ever seen an angel?

How do you think Joseph felt before the dream?

How did Joseph feel after the dream?

What do you think Joseph told Mary?

What do you think Mary was expecting Joseph to do when he discovered she was pregnant?

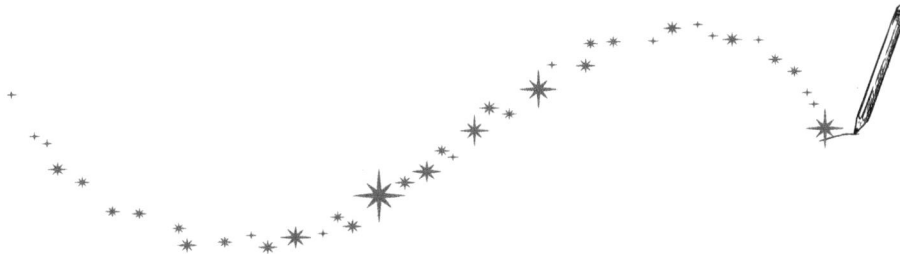

JESUS IS BORN

Luke 2:1-7

Imagine.

You are walking with a group of people on your way to Bethlehem, a little town at the edge of the desert. It's a long way and you must walk for many days to get there.

You have a job – you are in charge of Harry the donkey. You make sure you don't get too close to the back of the donkey; you don't want donkey poo on your shoes!

Harry is carrying Mary on his back. She is pregnant and is about to have her baby. You hope that the baby doesn't come before you get to Bethlehem! Joseph is leading Harry from the front. He looks back at Mary and smiles. You can tell that he loves her so much. You have heard him telling everyone about how the angel told them that they are going to have a little boy who they are going to name Jesus. You can't wait to meet Jesus. He must be a very special baby to have been talked about by the angels.

There are so many people going to Bethlehem. There is a Census on, which means that you and your family must go to Bethlehem so that you can be counted. You are related to King David. You are very proud of this. He was a great king and your Grandad has told you the story many times of how he killed the giant, Goliath.

Harry is getting a bit tired now; he needs a tap on his behind more often, to keep him moving forward.

"Come on Harry," you say, "we're nearly there. There's some nice fresh hay waiting for you in the stable."

Arriving in Bethlehem, there are so many tired, dusty people needing a bed and a bath. There are sheep bleating, cattle mooing, chickens squawking and your shoes definitely got some donkey poo on them. Joseph goes from door to door asking if anybody has a bed for him and his wife. Mary looks worried. You wonder if Jesus is going to be born very soon.

Joseph finds someone who offers them their stable to stay in. It smells of sheep and cows, but it's warm and Mary can lie down on the hay. You give Harry some hay outside the stable and he is soon chomping away happily. Joseph asks you to clean out the manger where a cow is licking up the last of her dinner. You have to lean up against the cow and push with all your might to move her. She objects to your pushes with a loud "Moooo!"

You want to meet Jesus, who you are sure will be born very soon. Outside the stable, Harry lies down, and you sit next to him, waiting expectantly for the time to come.

Your eyes are closing and you yawn. Then.....you hear a tiny baby's cry! Jumping up, you run into the stable to Mary and Joseph. Mary is gently holding Jesus in her arms.

She is smiling, but is very tired, so she hands the baby to Joseph who wraps Jesus up and places him gently in the manger. Walking around to the manger you watch Jesus sleep. He is so tiny.

"Hallo Jesus. I have been waiting to meet you for a long time." You lean over and kiss his head.

Talking Time

What was it like walking with the donkey, Joseph, and Mary?

What do you think Mary and Joseph felt when there was no room for them to stay in anybody's house?

How did it feel to be right there when Jesus was born?

What did you feel when you looked at Jesus lying in the manger?
What were you thinking?

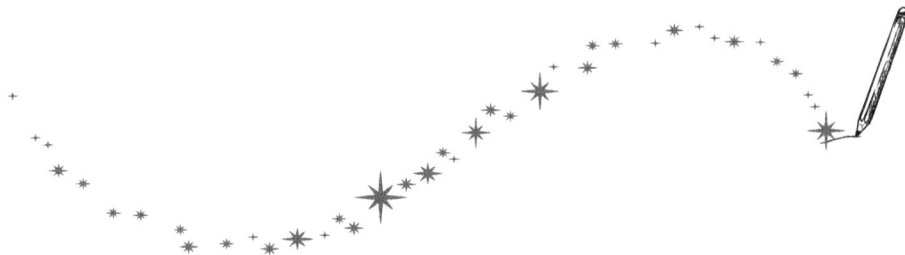

SHEPHERDS AND ANGELS

Luke 2:8-20

Imagine.

You are sitting in a field and the stars are starting to shine brightly in the night sky. Sitting around the campfire, listening to the fire crackling and feeling it warm your face, you and your friends are staring at one star in particular; it's much bigger and brighter than all the others and it seems to be shining over a stable far away in the distance, near the twinkling lights of the town of Bethlehem.

You all hear a loud bleating from a bush nearby. You jump up and run to see which of your sheep has got itself into trouble again. Being a shepherd is hard work!

Sure enough the usual culprit has got himself stuck in a thorn bush. You untangle the lamb from the thorns and put it back with its mother.

Suddenly, the darkness of the night is lit up as if it's daytime. You all jump with fright and run and hide amongst the sheep.

A voice speaks to you from the light, "Don't be afraid."

You peek over the woolly back of one of your sheep and you see a shining, golden angel of the Lord standing looking at you. The most beautiful light is shining out of him.

"I have come to bring you good news," the angel of the Lord reassures you and your friends, "the most happy news the world has ever heard!" And the angel laughs with joy.

You and your friends look at each, eyes wide with fright. Your heart is pounding in your chest. What could this news be?!

"Today, nearby in Bethlehem," the angel goes on to say, "a rescuer was born for you. He is the Messiah, the Lord. You will recognize Him by this miracle sign: You will find a baby wrapped in strips of cloth and lying in a manger."

Suddenly, the whole sky lights up. You look up and see the sky is filled with thousands and thousands and thousands of angels! They are all laughing and dancing and praising God, singing:

"Glory to God in the highest! For there is peace and a good hope given to the everyone!"

Just as suddenly as they had appeared, the angels disappear. Everything is quiet and dark again. Except for the bright star shining over the stable in the distance.

You and your friends cautiously look around to make sure it's safe and then you all turn and stare at the bright star and the stable in the distance.

Everyone starts shouting at once, "We have to go! Let's go! We have to see what the angels are so excited about. We have to see for ourselves what has happened that the Lord has told us about!!"

You tell your trusty sheepdog to stay and look after the sleeping sheep. Then you all go charging across the fields as fast as you can. You have never run so fast or felt so excited in your life!

You run through the village of Bethlehem, disturbing the quiet streets. Out of breath, you skid to a halt outside the stable opening.

You pause and take a deep breath before peeking inside and trying to be quiet.

Inside you see the light of a small fire; it's exactly as the angel of the Lord described it - Mary and Joseph and their new born baby, wrapped in strips of cloth and lying in the manger.

Mary sees you and whispers for you to come in. Quietly you walk over to the manger and look down at the baby.

"The angel of the Lord has told us that your baby boy is the Messiah!" You try to whisper, but you are so excited that your voice gets louder and louder as you tell Mary and Joseph about what just happened with the angels.

"Your baby's birth tonight is the best news the world has ever heard!"

You and your friends, with Mary and Joseph, just sit and stare at the sleeping Messiah and King. All that can be heard is the crackling of the fire and the snores of the sleeping donkey. You are filled with wonder and peace.

It's time to return to your sheep. You say goodbye to Mary and Joseph and Jesus and make your way back to the fields. The way back is much slower because you and your friends stop to tell everyone you meet about the angels and the best news about Jesus. Everyone is amazed.

Walking through the fields together, singing and dancing, you all feel so happy that the angels came and told you the news so that you could see Jesus yourself. It's the best news ever.

Finally, back at your campfire and your flock of sheep, you quickly drop off to sleep with a smile, dreaming of angels and bright stars.

Talking Time

What do you think the angel of the Lord looked like?

What do you think the angel choir sounded like?

Have you ever seen an angel?

What did you think when you sat quietly watching the baby Jesus sleep?

If you had the most important news ever to tell, who would you tell first?

What did you think and feel when the angels disappeared?

Where do you think the angels went when they disappeared?

Why do you think we can't see angels all the time?

THREE WISE MEN
SAVE KING JESUS

Matthew 2:1-12

Imagine.

You are an astronomer who studies the stars. You live in a country far from Jerusalem and you are known as a wise man.

You and your friends, who are also astronomers and wise men, have been keeping an eye on the stars for a very long time, waiting for a special one to appear.

One night as you sit watching the stars rise in the east, you notice a different star in the sky. This one is new! You run over to your friends and point excitedly at the new star.

"Could this be the one we have been expecting all these years? The one that will lead us to a powerful King born to the Jewish people?"

Amazed and excited you and your friends decide to follow the star to see this King of all kings; you want to bow down to him and to take him gifts.

"I bet King Herod can't be too pleased about this new King of the Jews," you exclaim.

You think of the best, most valuable gifts you can pack. You all gather together as much gold, frankincense, and myrrh you can find and load them onto your camels in huge treasure chests. This new King deserves all your wealth.

Arriving in Jerusalem after many months of travel, you ask around if anybody has heard of the birth of the King of the Jewish people. Nobody seems to know.

"Shhhhh…….I wouldn't spread that around!" one person warns you, "King Herod won't be too happy about that!"

Sure enough, you and your friends are commanded to go to the palace. You can tell that King Herod is shocked and horrified by the news that there is a new King.

"Where is this new King?" he demands to know.

"Maybe you could have a look in Bethlehem," one of his priests suggests.

"I remember reading that in the Jewish bible," someone else whispers.

"Off you go then," King Herod commands you impatiently, "go and find this new King so that I can go and worship Him." Hmmm……you wonder if he is telling the truth.

On your way to Bethlehem, you look up at the night sky as you usually do, and there is the star again!! It's big and bright and it's moving ahead of you, and amazingly, it stops directly over the place where the new King is! You didn't even have to ask anybody the way.

"Whoa!" you tell your camels to stop. Standing still and looking at the place where the star has stopped in the distance, you are all so happy. Everyone jumps off the camels and you start a dance party. Jumping, dancing and laughing, you have never felt this much joy ever!

Jumping back on your camels, you set out on the last little bit of your long journey. Finally!! You are going to see the King of kings.

Getting closer to the place where the star has stopped, you give each other a puzzled look. Could this be the right place? It's not very fancy; it's just an ordinary house. You steer your camels right up to the door of the house. You untie the treasure chests and with lots of huffing and puffing you unload the heavy gifts for King Jesus. The camels look relieved to be free of their heavy loads and they settle down for a rest.

You open the treasure chests and grab as many bags of gold and precious frankincense and myrrh as you can carry. Hmmm.....the frankincense smells amazing! The bags of gold are heavy!

You knock loudly and Joseph quickly opens the door. Oops, you hope you didn't wake King Jesus!

"Hallo!" Joseph is surprised to see such important visitors.

"We have followed the star all the way from the East to your house," you explain, pointing to the bright star shining above the house, "Please may we come inside to honour the baby boy who is the King of the Jews. We want to give him our gifts."

Joseph nods and leads you through the house to where Mary is playing with Jesus.

Bowing to your knees, you worship King Jesus, surrounding Him with your gifts. You notice the room fills with the smell of frankincense and myrrh and Jesus rubs his little nose and sneezes. Mary giggles. She and Joseph are very thankful for the valuable gifts.

Sleeping under the special star that night and listening to the camels chewing and snoring, you are grateful that you followed that star and made the long journey with your friends to worship King Jesus. You are certain that He is a very special King. You feel that you may need to protect Him, and so you say a prayer for Him before you drop off to sleep.

It's cold and still dark when you suddenly open your eyes, wide awake from a dream you just had. Throwing off your warm blanket, you rush over to your friends, shaking them awake.

"We have to go home another way! We can't go back to King Herod. He wants to hurt King Jesus. God told me in a dream!"

"He told me too!" says your friend.

"And me!" says another.

A little later you're all packed up and ready to go, saying goodbye to Mary and Joseph. You are sure that God will take care of them and protect them. He loves King Jesus very much.

Talking Time

Why did you want to go and worship the King of the Jewish people?

What did you feel when you saw the star moving to guide you to where Jesus was?

What was it like when you saw Jesus for the first time?

What did Jesus do when you gave him all those gifts?

What was it like to spend time with Jesus, Mary and Joseph?

What was it like when God warned you not to go back to Herod?

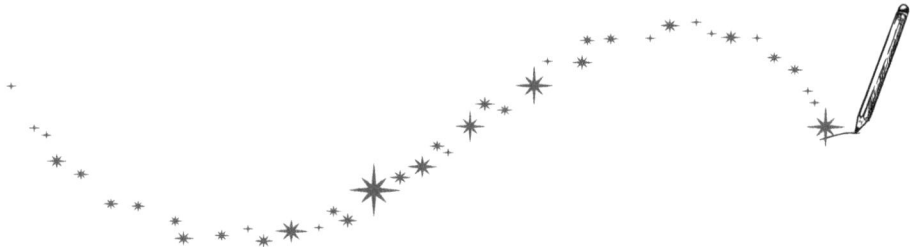

GRANDPA SIMEON AND THE BEST WEDNESDAY EVER

Luke 2:21-40

Imagine.

You live in Jerusalem with your family.

It's early, the sun is rising over the hills and, waking up, you remember it's Wednesday and..... it's the holidays! Excitedly you jump out of bed, quickly eat some breakfast, and bolt out the front door, almost forgetting to give your Mum a quick kiss goodbye.

Wednesday is the day you go and visit your grandpa Simeon. He, as usual, will go to the Temple where you get to hang out with your best friend Luca. Luca's grandma Anna is always in the Temple helping, worshipping God and praying. Luca told you one day that Grandma Anna is waiting for something very special to happen, but Luca's not sure what it is.

Grandpa Simeon lives just up the road. You quietly turn the knob and open his front door because grandpa Simeon is usually sitting talking to God and reading the Torah.

Surprise! Grandpa is ready to go! He greets you with a big smile and an even bigger hug. You love Grandpa's hugs.

Something amazing is going to happen today!" he says as he grabs his hat and your hand. Before you know it, you are outside again.

"What's the rush today, Grandpa?" you ask between breaths, hurrying to keep up. Grandpa Simeon usually moves slowly, but not today!

"Well, you know how I told you that God made me a promise?"

"Which one?" you ask.

"The most special one!" Grandpa answers.

Your heart skips a beat. "You mean the one about you won't die before you see the One Person you have been waiting and longing for - the Messiah?!"

"Yes, that very one!" He says, "God told me this morning that I will see him today. Hurry, hurry, my grandson, we don't want to miss Him." As you pick up the pace you are even more excited. This Wednesday is the most special Wednesday ever! You wonder if Luca's grandma Anna knows about the Messiah coming to the temple today. Maybe this is the special thing Grandma Anna has been waiting for all these years.

You and Grandpa dash up the stone steps to the heavy wooden temple door. Grandpa pushes it open and the two of you burst inside and look around. Everything appears to be normal. You spot Luca across the other side of the room. She looks up and excitedly runs over to you. Just as you are about to share the special news with her, a man and woman carrying a tiny bundle enter the temple. The tiny bundle is squirming, and you laugh when a small hand pops out of the blanket and tiny fingers tug at the dad's beard.

Grandpa Simeon seems to be holding his breath and is a little red-cheeked. He grasps your hand and slowly, and on trembling legs, he walks towards them. Is this what God has promised? The One he has been waiting for and longing to see all these years.

Luca seems to sense that something big is happening and instead of coming with you, you see her run over to her Grandma Anna and tug at her skirts and points at you and Grandpa.

"Good morning", the man says, "my name is Joseph, and this is my wife, Mary. This is our firstborn son and we have come to dedicate Him to God. We have named Him Jesus."

"May I?" Grandpa asks Joseph, looking with wonder at the baby in his arms. Joseph very gently, places their baby Son in Grandpa's arms.

Grandpa Simeon's face breaks into the biggest smile you have ever seen! Tears are streaming down his cheeks, tears of joy. Holding the sleeping baby Jesus in his arms, Grandpa lifts his face to heaven.

"Lord and Master, I am your servant," he prays, "and now I am content, for your promise to me has been fulfilled. With my own eyes I have seen the Saviour you have sent into the world."

He is talking about the baby he is holding in his arms! The promised Messiah.

Softly Grandma Anna begins to sing a beautiful song. The song fills the temple and as she sings everyone in the temple gathers round. Before long a great chorus of praise is echoing around the temple for this baby who is the Messiah, the Saviour of the whole world.

The song of praise fades and the temple goes quiet. Jesus opens his eyes and starts to wriggle. Grandpa kisses His forehead and blesses Him. He prays a special blessing over Mary and Joseph.

You and Luca look at each other both knowing that this is the best day EVER!!

You run off to play, talking about how you will invite Jesus to join in your games in the temple on Wednesdays when He is old enough.

Talking Time

Have you ever waited a long time for something?

What was it like when it finally happened?

What do you think Simeon felt like when he held the Messiah?

How do you think God told Simeon about him seeing Jesus?

Have you ever felt God share something with you?

How did He share with you?

What did He share with you?

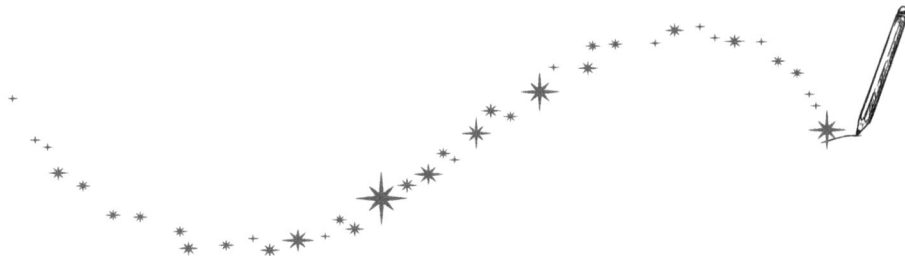

www.ingramcontent.com/pod-product-compliance
Lightning Source LLC
Chambersburg PA
CBHW040246100426
42811CB00011B/1168